D1196101

Wacky
BASKETBALL
TRIVIA

Fun Facts for Every Fan

By Matt Chandler

CAPSTONE PRESS
a capstone imprint

Sports Illustrated Kids Wacky Sports Trivia is published by Capstone Press,
1710 Roe Crest Drive, North Mankato, Minnesota 56003.
www.mycapstone.com

Library of Congress Cataloging-in-Publication Data
Library of Congress Cataloging-in-Publication data is on file at the Library
of Congress website.
ISBN 9781515719946 (library binding)
ISBN 9781515719984 (eBook PDF)

Editorial Credits
Brenda Haugen, editor; Terri Poburka, designer; Eric Gohl, media researcher;
Tori Abraham, production specialist

Photo Credits
Alamy: ZUMA Press, Inc., 28; AP Photo: Mark J. Terrill, 15 (top); Getty Images: Focus on
Sport, 15 (bottom), George Gojkovich, 9, Mitchell Layton, 14, NBAE/Andrew D. Bernstein,
18, NBAE/Danny Bollinger, 8; Shutterstock: 3DMI, 16 (shark), Dudarev Mikhail, 22 (cow),
GrandeDuc, cover, background (throughout), Hurst Photo, 12 (sandwich), Oleksiy Mark,
24 (pen); Sports Illustrated: Al Tielemans, 13, Bill Frakes, 23 (Obama), Bob Rosato, 4, 12
(Celtics), 25, Heinz Kluetmeier, 11, John Biever, 16 (Spurs), John D. Hanlon, 7, John Iacono,
26, 29, John W. McDonough, 10, 17, 24 (Bryant), 27, Manny Millan, 5, 6, 19, 20, 22–23
(Jordan), Walter Iooss Jr., 21

Printed in the United States of America.
032016   009682F16

Table of Contents

WACKY TIMES ON THE COURT

Lakers and Celtics, Pistons and Bulls, LeBron versus Steph. The National Basketball Association (NBA) is a league rich with **rivalries.** Some of the greatest athletes of all time have made their mark in the world of professional basketball. The NBA is a serious business, raking in more than $5.5 billion each year.

The Boston Celtics took on the Los Angeles Lakers in the 2008 NBA Finals.

But that doesn't mean there aren't plenty of goofballs in the league and plenty of bizarre stories from every team. Have you heard about the player who insists on sleeping in his opponent's shorts? Or the team that created a pregame **ritual** of eating a meal popular with small children? How about the future superstar **Hall of Famer** who was cut from his high school basketball team?

From quirky **superstitions** to oddball facts, wacky trivia puts hoops in a whole new light.

Charles Barkley and Grant Hill

rivalry—a fierce feeling of competition between two people or two teams

ritual—an action that is always performed in the same way

Hall of Fame—a place where people important to basketball are honored

superstition—a belief that an action or an object can affect the outcome of a future event

Chapter 1

HARDWOOD HEROES

The average NBA career lasts less than five seasons. The competition is fierce, and many players know they are only one injury or a bad season away from being out of a job. That's what makes some of these wacky trivia tales so interesting. It takes **persistence**, luck, and sometimes, unusual paths to make it to the NBA. Just ask this group of hardwood heroes.

★★★ NEVER GIVE UP ★★★

Charles Barkley was cut from his high school basketball team as a sophomore. Sir Charles overcame that early failure and went on to be selected in the first round of the NBA **draft**. He played 16 seasons, was an 11-time NBA **All-Star Game** selection, and won two Olympic gold medals.

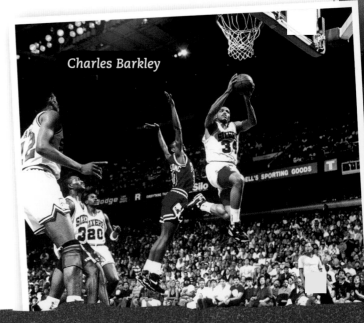

Charles Barkley

★★★ GLOBETROTTING TO THE NBA ★★★

Wilt Chamberlain ranks as one of the greatest players in the history of the NBA. His 31,419 points, 13 trips to the All-Star Game, and two NBA titles are proof of that. But Chamberlain wasn't an instant star in the NBA. He got his professional start playing for the Harlem Globetrotters. The goofy squad of entertainers that travel the world playing trick ball signed Chamberlain while he was in college. Reports say Chamberlain was paid about $50,000 for his one season with the team.

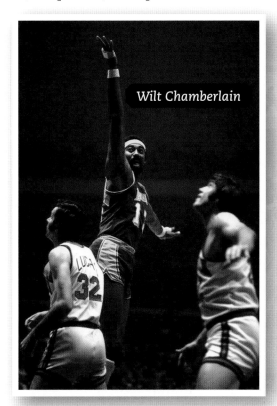

Wilt Chamberlain

persistence—to continue to work toward a goal, even when there are setbacks or challenges along the way

draft—an event in which athletes are picked to join sports organizations or teams

All-Star Game—a special game played every year in which the best NBA players play against one another

★★★ ADDICTED TO STRAWS? ★★★

Beginning when he was a teen, former first-round draft pick Caron Butler chewed drinking straws during games. During each NBA game, Butler would chew up a dozen straws. That was until he was traded to the Dallas Mavericks in 2010, and the NBA **banned** the practice. The league said Butler's habit was dangerous. Some of his teammates said it was plain weird. As for Butler, he said it helped him relax. But after Butler gave up the straws during games, he and his team won an NBA title.

Caron Butler

HE DIDN'T TRUST TIME ZONES
★ ★ ★

Marvin Barnes

Thanks to time zones, it's possible to take a short flight and land at an earlier local time than the time in the town you left behind. That was the case for former American Basketball Association (ABA) and NBA player Marvin Barnes. Barnes was set to board a flight with his team from Louisville, Kentucky, to St. Louis, Missouri. The 56-minute flight departed from the Eastern Time Zone and landed in the Central Time Zone. From the takeoff and landing times on the ticket, it appeared as if the flight would land four minutes before it took off. When Barnes saw the times on his ticket he said, "I ain't getting on no time machine." He rented a car and drove himself to St. Louis.

ban—to forbid something

Chapter 2

SUPERSTITIOUS SUPERSTARS

Like many athletes, some basketball players follow their own superstitions. Many NBA superstars practice elaborate pregame rituals—things they think help them play better on the court. Can eating the same meal before every game really make a person play better? Are any of these superstitions real? These NBA veterans sure think so.

STRANGE SLEEPWEAR
★ ★ ★

The night before every game, Jason Terry sleeps in a pair of shorts with his next opponent's logo. But Terry doesn't sleep in just any shorts. He gets them from a player on the other team. Does it bring him good luck? Well, Terry has played 17 seasons in the NBA for five teams, so maybe he's on to something.

Jason Terry

Michael Jordan

★★★ LUCKY SHORTS ★★★

As a guard with the University of North Carolina in 1982, Michael Jordan won a national championship. Jordan thought the shorts he wore were good luck, so he wore them for the next two decades. The Hall of Fame superstar won six NBA titles and two Olympic gold medals with his powder-blue college shorts under his NBA uniform.

★★★ PBJ TIME ★★★

The Boston Celtics have won a record 17 NBA titles. But only one, the 2008 crown, included a pregame ritual of eating peanut butter and jelly sandwiches. It began with the arrival of superstar Kevin Garnett, who ate a PB&J before every game. Soon it caught on among his teammates as a must-have before tip-off. The Celtics sandwich superstition was so big, the locker room had a jelly divide—grape or strawberry.

Boston Celtics (from left) Kevin Garnett, Paul Pierce, and Ray Allen celebrate the 2008 championship.

Shaquille O'Neal attempts a free throw shot as Philadelphia 76ers fans wave objects in hopes of making him miss.

★★★ FREE THROW FAILURE ★★★

Shaquille O'Neal ranked as one of the most dominant big men in the NBA in the 1990s—except when it came to shooting free throws. Shaq was a disaster from the foul line. Did a superstition lead to Shaq missing more than 5,300 free throws in his career? The free throw is all about routine. Players hold the ball the same way and bounce it the same number of times before they shoot. They create a rhythm and repeat it. Not Shaq. He believed if he missed a foul shot, the answer was to change his mechanics for the next shot. He might bend his knees more, arc the ball higher, or change how he gripped the ball. It was an odd belief, and one that never worked. Shaq shot just 52.7 percent from the line for his career, making him one of the worst free throw shooters ever to play the game.

Chapter 3

A WACKY MIX OF WILD STORIES

Thousands of players have played in the NBA and the Women's National Basketball Association (WNBA). The best are legends, but plenty are quickly forgotten. The men and women in this chapter all found unusual ways to leave their mark on the game. Some set records on the court, others off the court, and for one player, it took a bizarre storm to land him in the NBA. Being an NBA scout and predicting who is the best player in the draft can be a wacky job too.

Heather Burge

★★★ TALLEST TWINS ★★★

Though their WNBA careers were short, sisters Heidi and Heather Burge earned a spot in the Guinness Book of World Records. In 1991 Guinness recognized the Burges as the tallest living identical twin sisters, each standing 6 feet 5 inches

(196 centimeters) tall. Their reign at the top lasted until 2004 when sisters Ann and Claire Recht measured in at 6 feet 7 inches (201 cm) tall.

Heidi Burge

TWO EXTREMES, ONE TEAM
★ ★ ★

The shortest and the tallest players to ever play in the NBA were once teammates. Muggsy Bogues holds the record as the shortest man to ever play in the NBA. Bogues stood just 5 feet 3 inches (160 cm) tall. That's almost 2.5 feet (76 cm) shorter than the league's tallest player, the 7-foot-7-inch (231-cm) Manute Bol. The two were teammates for a single season with the 1987 Washington Bullets.

★★★ THANK THE SHARKS ★★★

Tim Duncan has five NBA championship rings and has been named league **MVP** twice. He's a lock for the Hall of Fame when his playing days are over. But if it wasn't for a hurricane, Duncan might never have played basketball. Growing up on the island of St. Croix, Duncan was a standout swimmer with dreams of going to the Olympics. But in 1989 Hurricane Hugo struck the island, and the pool Duncan used for training was destroyed. Duncan's team had no choice but to move their practices to the ocean. The teenaged Duncan was so terrified of sharks and the ocean itself, he refused to go in the water. His fear of sharks led him to take up basketball, and the rest is history.

Tim Duncan

★★★ LONG-RANGE TROUBLE ★★★

Former Lakers superstar Shaquille O'Neal only sank one three-point shot in 19 seasons. Shaq launched nearly 20,000 shots from the field during his Hall of Fame career. But the big man attempted only 22 shots from long-range. He played 15 seasons without sinking one after his lone three-point bucket during the 1995–96 season.

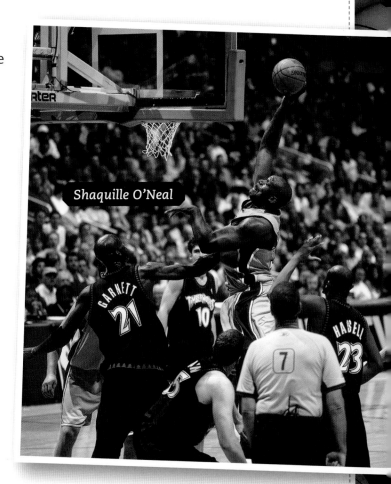

Shaquille O'Neal

MVP—stands for Most Valuable Player; an honor given to the best player in a tournament or during a season

Kobe Bryant

DRAFT DISASTER
★ ★ ★

Professional scouts get paid to **evaluate** players in high school and college and decide who is the best. In 1996 a teenager named Kobe Bryant was drafted by the Charlotte Hornets. Today Bryant is considered one of the best players in the history of the NBA. Yet in 1996, scouts didn't see him as a No. 1 pick. Bryant went 13th in the draft. Lorenzen Wright, Kerry Kittles, Samaki Walker, Erick Dampier, Todd Fuller, and Vitaly Potapenko were among those drafted ahead of Bryant. Bryant certainly proved the scouts wrong. His 33,464 career points are 5,593 points more than the combined total of those six players.

★★★ DRAFT DISAPPOINTMENT ★★★

Byrant may have dropped to 13 in the NBA draft, but not a single team was interested in drafting former Oklahoma State University guard John Starks in 1988. But that didn't stop Starks. He played in the Continental Basketball Association and the World Basketball League before getting his big break with the New York Knicks. Starks went on to score more than 10,000 points, dish more than 3,000 **assists**, and collect more than 2,000 rebounds. Not bad for a guy nobody wanted.

John Starks

evaluate—to judge or determine the value of someone or something

assist—a pass that leads to a score by a teammate

★★★ NO EXPERIENCE REQUIRED ★★★

Carl Lewis was a world-class track and field athlete who won nine Olympic gold medals. Lewis was an incredible athlete, but he never played a single game of basketball in high school or college. That didn't stop the Chicago Bulls from selecting Lewis in the 1984 NBA draft, but Lewis never played in the NBA.

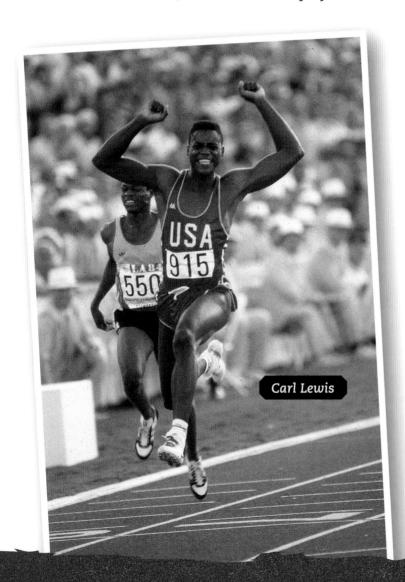

Carl Lewis

ONE OF A KIND
★ ★ ★

The selection of track athlete Carl Lewis by the Bulls made headlines around the world. But his selection isn't the most unique pick in the history of the NBA draft. In 1977 the New Orleans Jazz selected Delta State's Lusia Harris in the seventh round of the draft. Seventh-round picks rarely drew much attention, but Harris was the first and only woman ever drafted by an NBA team. She chose not to sign with the Jazz and later played one season of professional basketball with the Houston Angels of the Women's Professional Basketball League (WBL).

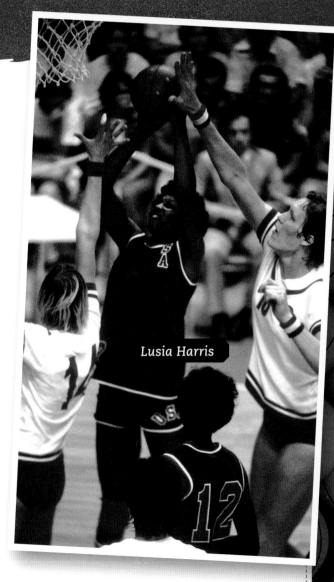
Lusia Harris

Chapter 4

FROM DUNKS TO DRESSERS

Basketball is a game driven by statistics—shots, points, rebounds, and steals. While stats are an important part of the game, some of the wackiest trivia related to the game never shows up on the postgame stat sheets. From counting cows to counting votes, there are some weird and wild stories off the court.

★★★ COWS ON THE COURT ★★★

The NBA switched to a ball made with a **synthetic** cover about 10 years ago, but before then every ball was made of leather. Twelve NBA basketballs could be made from a single cowhide. It took 180 cattle to make the game balls for a single season. That's not counting the hundreds of balls teams have for practice. That's a lot of beef!

★★★ PRESIDENTIAL SUPERSTITION ★★★

In 2008 then-Senator Barack Obama played basketball on the day that Iowa held its presidential **caucus**, and he won.

President Barack Obama

From Iowa, Senator Obama traveled to New Hampshire and prepared for that state's primary vote. Obama didn't play ball on primary day and lost. From that point forward, he made sure to shoot hoops on every voting day, and he rode the round ball to the White House … twice!

synthetic—something that is made by people rather than found in nature

caucus—a meeting of members of a political party during which they select a candidate to support for office

★★★ PARENTAL SUPPORT ★★★

In his final NBA season, future Hall of Famer Kobe Bryant earned a salary of $25 million. Bryant earned a cool $680 million in his career. Not bad for a guy who wasn't even legally allowed to sign his first **contract**. When the Charlotte Hornets drafted Bryant in 1996, he was just 17 years old. A player must be 18 to legally sign a contract. Bryant was traded to the Lakers shortly after the draft, and his mom and dad had to sign his first pro contract to make it a legal document.

Kobe Bryant

★★★ "BIG BABY," BIG BUCKS ★★★

Former Celtic power forward Glen Davis had a unique nickname. Teammates called him "Big Baby," a name that dated back to his childhood. But Davis' nickname isn't the wackiest bit of trivia about him. During his playing days, Davis tipped the scales at close to 300 pounds (136 kilograms). The Celtics were concerned that Davis' size could lead to an increased risk of injury or poor performance. When it came time for Davis to sign a new contract, the Celtics management added an unusual **incentive**. Davis was required to weigh in at different points of the season. If he kept his weight below a certain number for the season, he would earn an extra $500,000. Though the agreed-upon weight was kept a secret, David had a half-million reasons to stick to his diet.

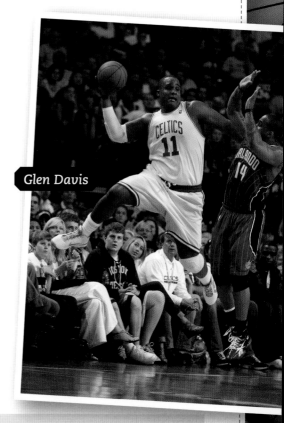
Glen Davis

contract—a legal agreement between people stating the terms by which one will work for the other

incentive—something that makes a person try or work harder

★★★ $5,000 SNEAKERS? ★★★

Off the court, Michael Jordan is best known for his incredibly popular sneakers, Nike Air Jordans. The man whose name is on the biggest-selling sneaker in history wasn't supposed to wear his kicks when the original Jordans were introduced in 1985. The commissioner of the NBA banned the shoes, and Jordan was fined $5,000 every game that he wore them on the court. Nike happily paid the fine for Jordan.

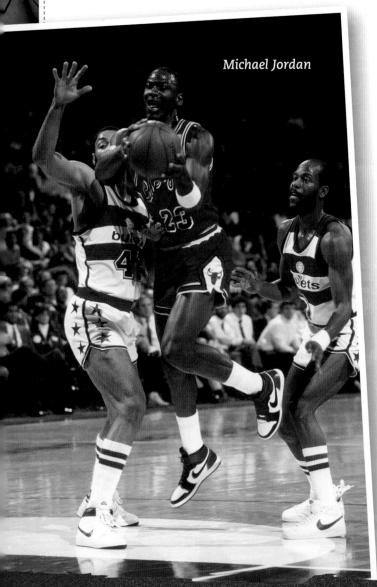

Michael Jordan

★★★ GETTING PAID WHEN YOU CAN'T PLAY ★★★

Many NBA players took their game overseas during the 2011 NBA **lockout**, while others relaxed at home on the couch. Former NBA guard Delonte West may have even delivered the couch. Though he earned more than $14 million playing in the NBA, West decided to earn some cash by working in a furniture warehouse while the NBA was shut down. The lockout eventually ended, and West resumed his career with the Dallas Mavericks, giving his warehouse coworkers a pretty cool story to tell their friends.

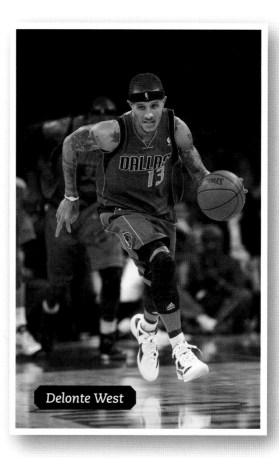

Delonte West

> **lockout**—a period of time in which owners prevent players from reporting to their teams; owners do not pay players during a lockout

★★★ A SOMETIMES GOOFY GAME ★★★

Fans love basketball because it is fast-paced, high scoring, and intense. But beyond the dribbling, dunks, and dynamic plays on the court, there are many wacky elements that make basketball such a fun game to be a fan of. For example, off the court Shaq starred in both a Disney movie and a rap music video.

Shaquille O'Neal

Michael Jordan

Michael Jordan quit basketball mid-career to play professional baseball. And then there was the time Lakers rookie Larry Nance Jr. scored on a beautiful one-handed jump shot—for the other team!

No team has ever won the NBA title because they had the wackiest players or the craziest stories. But the colorful personalities and goofy tales can add to the fun and excitement of any basketball game.

★ Glossary ★

All-Star Game (AWL-star GAYM)—a special game played every year in which the best NBA players play against one another

assist (uh-SIST)—a pass that leads to a score by a teammate

ban (BAN)—to forbid something

caucus (CAW-cuss)—a meeting of members of a political party during which they select a candidate to support for office

contract (KAHN-trakt)—a legal agreement between people stating the terms by which one will work for the other

draft (DRAFT)—an event in which athletes are picked to join sports organizations or teams

evaluate (i-VAL-yoo-ayt)—to judge or determine the value of someone or something

Hall of Fame (HAWL UV FAYM)—a place where people important to basketball are honored

incentive (in-SEN-tiv)—something that makes a person try or work harder

lockout (LOK-owt)—a period of time in which owners prevent players from reporting to their teams; owners do not pay players during a lockout

MVP (EM-VEE-PEE)—stands for Most Valuable Player; an honor given to the best player in a tournament or during a season

persistence (pur-SIS-tuhns)—to continue to work toward a goal, even when there are setbacks or challenges along the way

ritual (RICH-oo-uhl)—an action that is always performed in the same way

rivalry (RYE-vuhl-ree)—a fierce feeling of competition between two people or two teams

superstition (soo-pur-STI-shuhn)—a belief that an action or an object can affect the outcome of a future event

synthetic (sin-THET-ik)—something that is made by people rather than found in nature

★ Read More ★

Chandler, Matt. *The Science of Basketball: The Top 10 Ways Science Affects the Game.* Top 10 Science. North Mankato, Minn.: Capstone Press, 2016.

Omoth, Tyler. *Who's Who of Pro Basketball: A Guide to the Game's Greatest Players.* Sports Illustrated Kids Who's Who of Pro Sports. North Mankato, Minn.: Capstone Press. 2016.

Schaller, Bob, and Dave Harnish. *The Everything Kids' Basketball Book: The All-Time Greats, Legendary Teams, Today's Superstars—and Tips on Playing Like a Pro.* Avon, Mass.: Adams Media, 2015.

★ Internet Sites ★

FactHound offers a safe, fun way to find Internet sites related to this book. All of the sites on FactHound have been researched by our staff.

Here's all you do:

Visit *www.facthound.com*

Type in this code: 9781515719946

 Check out projects, games and lots more at
www.capstonekids.com

★ Index ★